The Sabal Palm

A Native Monarch

Barbara Oehlbeck

FIRST EDITION

To see the first noble palmetto growing wild on the bank of a river is an event in one's life, but to behold groups and forests of them is like a miracle.

They form pictures of enchanting scenery in the soul of the lover of nature which are indelibly impressed as long as life lasts. . . .

A single well-developed specimen with its massive trunk and dense leaf crown is a most beautiful object, but far more effective are groups and masses of a hundred or more. They simply defy description.

DR. HENRY NEHRLING
MY GARDEN IN FLORIDA, 1946

The
SABAL
PALM

A Native Monarch

Barbara Oehlbeck

Gulfshore Press

The Sabal Palm

A Native Monarch

Published by Gulfshore Press

A division of Gulfshore Communications

2975 South Horseshoe Drive, Suite 100

Naples, Florida 34104

Library of Congress Cataloging-in-Publication Data

Oehlbeck, Barbara H., 1925-
      The Sabal Palm, A Native Monarch
      1. Natural history—plants 2. Ethnobotany—
      Florida Indians
I. Title
ISBN 0-9654019-0-1: $19.95

Book Design by Rick Bopp
Printed in the United States of America

For The Captain,

Who made the grand pronouncement as we sped southward above the broad expanse of the St. Mary's River: "There she is—Florida—with more flowers and trees than even you can imagine." And then, touching my hand, he said, "The word Florida means 'the land of flowers.'"

We had not spanned the river before I asked about the shaggy, bronze and green palms growing along the highway and scattered across wandering savannas stretching east and west. "The sabal palm," he replied, "which will be our state tree as soon as we become residents."

As quickly as the law allowed, we became residents of this land of flowers, but even more quickly, we came to know and appreciate Florida's state tree. And the more we learned, the more concerned we became about *Sabal palmetto,* the cabbage palm.

ACKNOWLEDGMENTS

More than five years ago, I had almost given up on this book. After trying repeatedly to find it the right niche, there was no perfect fit. So on the winter day when I first spoke with Marjory Stoneman Douglas about my manuscript, I was discouraged and frustrated.

But she graciously invited me to visit her at home to discuss the work. There, sitting at her knees on a small stool in her living room/library, I read the manuscript to her (her sight was then failing) while she listened carefully, making gentle suggestions and comments. When I was finished, she offered to write the introduction.

To say that I was grateful, and to offer her a simple thank-you is totally inadequate. The fact is, without her inspiring encouragement—typical of her and of the lifelong crusade she has led for the natural communities of Florida—this book might well have been abandoned.

Perhaps in years to come, there will be those who silently or otherwise will be grateful for every tree she has saved and every bird that did not die because of her unwavering efforts to save the very soul of Florida.

And there are many others to whom I am more than simply grateful, although it is not possible to name them in order of importance: to The Captain, for putting up with everything all of this took (with pure grace) and for not ever being sorry for showing me the first sabal palm I ever laid my eyes upon.

To Chief James Billie for inviting me, and the public, into his private woodland world to see and feel his extraordinary love and devotion for the Indians' *Shee-lah-mah-shee-kee Tahl-cho-bee*—the sabal palm—the cabbage tree—their tree of life.

To Gulfshore Press' vice president and publisher, Ty Smith, for his "real good" listening; editor Amy Bennett who truly believed in the work and for her editing skills, and to my friend Sara Williams who led me there.

To the distinguished Drs. Margaret and Walton Gregory, who not only critiqued the work for botanical accuracy, but indexed the book as well, and guided me through deeper swamps than could be forded alone!

To Peter Burner, who marches at the head of the parade, lauding and applauding "the matriarch" of the natural Florida landscape. His conclusion is a paean of dedicated appreciation and admiration for *Sabal palmetto.* To Bill Hammond, who calls our state tree an uncommon natural wonder; to Richard Workman, who from our first meeting when signing his own book, *Growing Native,* for me, has steadfastly demonstrated belief in and patience for all my work, and for bringing this book to a poetic—and perhaps prophetic—close.

To Teresa Artuso, who advocates the use of and care for this native monarch in her work as a landscape architect; to John Franklin Pearce for not only caring enough to translocate sabals as shade for cattle in his own vast pastures in Glades County, Florida, but for relating a lifetime of stories about the tree he grew up with, and to Dr. Cooper Abbott for permission to use his extensive research and material about chickees.

Thanks also to Val Martin/Florida Classics Library for permission to use various passages from some of their books and for the encouragement to "keep on keepin' on!"; to Sam Mickler of Mickler's Floridiana for his constant support and being enthusiastically anxious to list this book among his other Florida titles; to Mona Ives of Ives Book Store for constantly exploring and researching ways to reach the final goal—and always with cheer and honesty.

I am most grateful to John Briggs for his spectacular painting on the dust jacket; to Clyde Butcher for generously allowing the use of his lyrical photos; to Dr. Robin Brown for his gracious permission to use his ethnobotanical photos; to Kent Jager for his striking photo of the flicker; to artist and native Floridian Anne Patterson Friedman, for her love and appreciation of the natural world and her ability to reflect that in her art; and to nephew (and all but a son) C.C. F. Gachet, who made a special trip from his home in Pennsylvania to the wilds of Grassy Run to photograph "Sabals at Sunset" as well as the cardinal's penthouse in Lyke's fire tower in Muse.

If someone has been omitted, forgive me—it is not intentional.

Barbara Oehlbeck

CONTENTS

INTRODUCTION

This work represents dedicated appreciation and study, as well as love and honor for the gifts of nature that man cannot enhance, nor replace. It also represents a deep and abiding knowledge of the fact that once these gifts are lost, they cannot be restored. Trees are among these gifts—in this instance, *Sabal palmetto,* the state tree of Florida and South Carolina.

We who are concerned with ecological preservation must be constantly reminded that when one link in the exquisite and fragile chain of the environment is lost, the entire length is weakened. When nature deals herself a disastrous blow, she instinctively and efficiently heals herself. Yet, when man erupts and manipulates various components of nature, the parts, the components die—over which, nature has no control.

Had the Kissimmee River been recognized for its role in the overall environmental structure, Lake Okeechobee would not be dying, and had the lake been recognized as vital to the natural ecology of the Everglades, this vast river of grass, unlike any other in the world, and the wildlife that called the Everglades home, would still be with us, relatively unaltered.

Even in the light of restoration, the channelization of the Kissimmee River was a horrendously expensive undertaking with monumental damages from which the land, the river, its tributaries, wetlands and the wildlife that the region supported, can never fully recover. The restoration effort is commendable and must, of course, be expedited, *but we must learn that the environmental system of the universe works as it was created.* We must stop trying to make the earth over to suit the special interests of every new generation!

An older contemporary of Confucius, Lao Tsu, wrote: "Do you think you can take over the universe and improve it? I do not believe it can be done. The universe is sacred. You cannot improve it. If you try to change it, you will ruin it."

It is thoroughly arrogant for us, as individuals, or groups, to assume that we can re-design and improve the way the earth is put together.

Barbara Oehlbeck's study of *Sabal palmetto* demonstrates clearly the major role the state tree of Florida has played in the lives of her people for hundreds of years. Now, while the tree still grows in abundance, is the time to bring the awareness of the palm's importance to the forefront, and to keep it there where it belongs, in order that it does not become endangered. The purpose at the heart of this work is to awaken to public knowledge the fact that if we keep on destroying the sabal—or any of Nature's vital parts—we will wake up one day to find that it is no longer growing in abundance.

Fifty years ago, who would ever have believed channelizing the meandering Kissimmee River would lead to the eutrophication of a lake as large as Okeechobee—that the intensive

MARJORY STONEMAN
DOUGLAS WITH FLORIDA
GOVERNOR LAWTON CHILES

drainage, subsequent agricultural development south of the lake together with subsidization of the sugar industry would lead to such disastrous fires and drought in the Everglades National Park?

The future for South Florida, as for all once-beautiful and despoiled areas of our country, lies in aroused and informed public opinion and citizen action.

The answer is preservation.

Preservation on the part of developers. Preservation on the part of individuals, both residents and tourists, and preservation on the part of the State of Florida. Half of the region of the Everglades has already been lost to development and pollution, and if the pace continues, the 'Glades—indeed all South Florida—could become a desert. We cannot be complacent, even about a tree that may seem to some common.

Sabal palmetto, the cabbage palm, is a treasure that belongs to the entire State of Florida, and should be respected and preserved as such.

Marjory Stoneman Douglas

2

A Note to the Reader

As governor of the great Palmetto State, it is my distinct pleasure to be included in Barbara Oehlbeck's book, *The Sabal Palm, A Native Monarch.*

One of the most distinctive features of our beautiful South Carolina landscape is the *Sabal palmetto,* which Mrs. Oehlbeck has chosen to celebrate in this intensive study. South Carolinians are especially proud of the palmetto as our state tree, which stands as a proud and glorious symbol of the noble character of our people and our land.

Not only has the palmetto been a vital resource to South Carolinians throughout our history, but its beauty is also commemorated today on our state flag and the name of our state's highest honor

THE GOVERNOR'S SEAL
OF SOUTH CAROLINA

for service, the Order of the Palmetto. Even as South Carolina's economy continues to experience tremendous growth, we remain committed to responsible stewardship of our God-given natural resources, most notably of our beloved palmetto.

I commend Mrs. Oehlbeck for her beautiful representation of this most cherished symbol of South Carolina's natural abundance. It is my hope that *The Sabal Palm, A Native Monarch* will enrich the lives of all who read it and will serve as a valuable resource in the ongoing efforts to preserve the pristine beauty of our land.

David M. Beasley

David M. Beasley was elected governor of South Carolina in 1994.

PART I

CHAPTER ONE

AN ENDURING BEAUTY

The nature of a native monarch

To a stranger, the cabbage palm may resemble a rough-hewn utility pole topped with a huge, floppy dust mop. Yet this is one of the most versatile trees in North America.

None of the world's 2,500 or so palm species grows in as many geographical areas or conditions as does the sabal. It thrives in vast open prairies and dry sand ridges, along wide rivers and shady streams, in the peaty dark soils of subtropical hammocks, on coastal shell mounds and behind ocean dunes. In some places, nature has swept the cabbage palm into winding ribbon patterns between swamps; in others, she has tucked them into fragrant pine woods.

In tidy street plantings and stylized parks, in pastures and forests, the sabal palm can live happily in dense clusters or in close company with two or three others of its kin, but sabal palms also are frequently seen growing as solitary giants—a weathered symbol of the survival of the fittest.

The tree's scientific name is *Sabal palmetto* (pronounced SAY-bal palm-EH-tow). The word *Sabal* is of unknown origin; *palmetto* comes from the Latin for the palm of the hand and refers to the shape of the fronds, or leaves. Commonly, it's known interchangeably as the sabal palm and the cabbage palm or tree—not because of the way it looks, but because the tree's tender heart can be harvested and cooked into a dish known as swamp cabbage or heart of palm.

Because the sabal palm is home for so many wild animals and plants, and because it has been so important to many of the indigenous peoples in its range, some refer to is as "the tree of life." It's also sometimes called the "vine tower" of the forest, because no other tree invites as many vines to seek their place in the sun as the sabal palm. As the official state tree of both Florida and South Carolina, *Sabal palmetto* is perhaps the South's best-known native palm.

Palms are a curious breed; more closely related to plants like grasses and lilies than to trees like oaks and pines. They are monocots—flowering plants with only one seed leaf. In both design and architecture, nature's construction of the palms is far different from that of the enormous class of branching trees. With no limbs and no annual growth rings, a young palm tree slowly attains its adult diameter. Once it does, the trunk, which contains soft, fibrous pith, does not get thicker as the tree grows taller. Even though the average height of *Sabal palmetto* is about 50 feet, they can

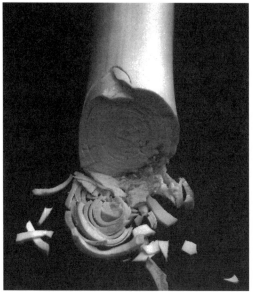

THE HEART OF THE SABAL PALM IS ALSO KNOWN AS SWAMP CABBAGE. CUTTING IT KILLS THE TREE.

PHOTO COURTESY ROBIN BROWN

get quite a bit taller. The tallest *Sabal palmetto* documented in the United States by the American Forestry Association (which keeps an official register of the nation's largest trees by species) is a 63-foot tall specimen in Georgia. Florida's state champion, measured in Lafayette County in 1994, is 60 feet tall, with a 69-inch circumference and a crown diameter of 16 feet. However, people familiar with the sabal palm will tell you that they often grow far taller, and that 70- and 80-foot tall specimens can be found—they just have to be officially recorded before they can unseat the reigning champions.

The sabal palm's fronds, or leaves, are produced from a single growth point, a cabbage-like bud in the center of the crown at the top of the stem. This bud is critical—and dangerously vulnerable. As it goes, so goes the tree. Destruction of the bud kills the palm. Man's delight in the taste of the sabal palm bud is fatal to the tree.

The rounded, compact head, seven to 12 feet wide, is composed of stiff, deeply cut fronds that curve outward and downward. This curved leaf stalk extends through the frond's fan, giving it a distinct midrib. Botanists call this frond type costapalmate. The trunk is usually single and straight, stout and rough.

Sabal palm flowers emerge from among the leaf stems. When they mature, the buds burst open with a soft swoosh, releasing a great cluster of cream-colored, sweet-smelling flowers, heavily endowed with nectar, which bees use to make some of the region's most sought-after honey. Butterflies also feed on sabal palm nectar, sipping up the minuscule droplets that form on the branched inflorescence. The tree's fruit—dull, black, pea-size berries that surround a hard seed—follow the flowers. After a season of aging, the hulls that encase the seeds become hard and durable. The large, wiry growths that house the seeds cling to the palm's crown until wind, rain or new growth fell them. Sometimes squirrels, leaping from frond to frond along their private sabal skyway, send these broom-like structures

HIGHLAND HAMMOCK #1
CLYDE BUTCHER

8

crashing to ground.

The sabal palm's dense, ropy root system clings tenaciously to whatever purchase it can find, even to rock and coral formations in coastal locations. The cabbage palm does not seem to care whether or not its roots are dry or wet, as long as the situation is not solely one or the other all year. It does well close to hardwood hammocks (from the Arawak Indian word *hamaca*—islands of trees amidst savannas), where there may be a spring or no trace of water at all. It is not unusual for these hammocks to be so thickly entwined with vines that walking through one is impossible without a brush-cutter of some sort.

And, although the sabal palm prefers a subtropical climate, it is one of the few palms that has come to limited terms with cold weather, and stubbornly survives where temperatures often plunge to far below freezing. There is one such example in Hickory, North Carolina, northwest of Charlotte, in the lower Appalachian Mountains. Another species of *Sabal (Sabal minor)* grows as far north as Missouri.

Throughout its range, *Sabal palmetto* exhibits an enduring beauty that is all the more extraordinary because it is as everyday as the fragrant piney woods. All year long, its handsome silvered greens, often awash with golden brown, never lose their luster. Standing tall, straight and strong, perhaps a bit disheveled, yet always regal, the sabal's spring and summer dress is various shades of fern-green with gleaming silver overtones, while its mid-winter attire is diverse hues of golden-brown and olive-green. Subtly, season to season, the lower fronds deepen from golden-green to rich, brown tones until finally, they become completely dry.

Being generally a tidy tree, the brittle dry fronds break off, leaving a fretwork of snapped stem-ends known as "boots," or "bootjacks." Trunks encased by boots have a precisely plaited appearance. On some trees, after tenaciously hugging the trunk for years, the boots slough off, leaving virtually no sign that they were ever there except for a slight, scar-like ring. It is not known why some trees naturally shed their boots, while others die of old age with their boots on.

Because the boots protrude more or less at right angles from the trunk, the cabbage palm is also known as the ladder tree, and man or beast can easily use the stairstep pattern of the boots as footholds to scale the trunk. From the base to the bud, joints of bootjacks at the trunk remain secure and strong for a considerable time after the frond has broken off at the neck.

It is a rarity to see a sabal palm with a branched trunk, although they do exist; there are at least two with twin trunks in Southwest Florida. One is on Sanibel Island at the fire station, another lives on State Road 80 near the Orange River bridge in east Lee County.

Even more of a rarity is a sabal palm with more than two trunks, and it is also rather unusual to see *Sabal palmetto* with a distinctively curved trunk, for its natural tendency is to grow straight. Yet at times, Mother Nature throws the tree a handsome curve: the wake of a river or creek can undermine the root system, causing the tree to lean. Or another tree, falling on the sabal's trunk will knock the sabal down horizontally, after which, the palm may cling to the soil with whatever roots remain.

Eventually, the sun again draws the head of the palm skyward, and the trunk will curve accordingly. However, from time to time, in an open prairie, and for no apparent reason, sabals develop remarkably curved trunks that give them a striking resemblance to the coconut palm.

CHAPTER TWO

THE TREE OF LIFE

Wild creatures and the sabal palm

Since its birth on the North American continent, who knows how many eons ago, the sabal palm has offered a well-stocked supply house for home-builders of all sorts. What's more, the cabbage palm serves as a real estate developer as well, providing an extraordinary variety of home sites with all sorts of amenities.

Wild creatures that use the sabal palm for construction materials or shelter include mammals, birds, reptiles, amphibians and insects, who take advantage of the tree's bounty from the tips of its silver-green fronds to the sturdy base of its trunk.

One of the most fastidious and exacting in its selection of construction materials is the hummingbird. This tiny bird's nest is an exquisitely dainty and artistic structure, and its builders are extremely selective not only with building materials, but for the site as well. Hummingbirds do not build in close proximity to others of their kind; they are

11

very private little creatures, not requiring close friends and neighbors.

For their tiny cup-like house, hummers seek the softest down or fuzzy materials they can find. Several varieties of ferns with furry surfaces grow readily in the boots of sabals, as do numbers of air plants whose seed pods are filled with a downy substance. When hummingbirds find a source of suitable nest-making materials, they exhibit an amazing strength in pulling the materials out and away from the host plant. Whether the nest is composed of fragments of fern fronds, the soft, fibrous material at the base of the sabal palm boots, cattail fluff, bits of grass and leaves, small feathers, or a combination, the entire structure is knit firmly together with spider webs, of which *Sabal palmetto* offers an unending supply. The webs also act as cement to fasten the nest to its support beam, whatever that happens to be.

It is not enough for a hummingbird to simply build a sturdy nest to hold her eggs and house her nestlings, it must also be decorated on the outside. This is accomplished with tiny bits of moss and lichens that the birds find readily on the trunks of many sabal palms, particularly those in hammocks or near water.

Although many hummingbirds select a building site in the highest branches of trees, it is not unusual for these tiniest of avian architects to glue their penthouse nest to a cabbage palm frond, the ribs of the frond acting as an anchor. In such cases, the nest takes on a sharply conical shape, not unlike an ice cream cone, following the ribs or lines of the frond itself. After Mother Hummer completes her outside decoration with grayish-green lichens and tiny tufts of moss, the structure is magnificently camouflaged. In almost all instances, the hummer's building site is selected beneath a living leaf, which provides an efficient roof for the nest and its wee inhabitants.

It might be said that the condominium concept originated with the cabbage palm. The precisely positioned boot units rise much as stories of an apartment building do, affording accommodations to many trunk-dwellers. Mother Nature's amenities in the little boot units and balconies include safety from wind, rain and searing sun. For most occupants, there is considerable food within reach: the fruit of the palm itself, the berries of the various vines that wrap themselves around the trunk, plus the myriad insects that come and go constantly. Drinks are often served "on the house," as rain and other moisture collect on the leaves and are funneled to the center bud, where they sustain animals and plants alike. And all the rooms—being situated on the radial perimeter of the "building"—boast a view.

Occupants include the many bird species that make their nests high among the hidden branches, squirrels, raccoons, various snakes, frogs, lizards, insects, and a handful of burrowing creatures that prefer basement apartments—dens among the ropy roots.

A fascinating family of flora makes its home in the crown of the leaves and among the bootjacks of cabbage palms. One such plant is the ancient whisk fern, *Psilotun nudum*, a plant that is not a fern at all, but is actually the most primitive of all vascular plants. It tends to anchor itself to the sabal palm, letting its mop of long, slender, deep green leaves hang down in such a way that it resembles a whisk broom.

It seems inconceivable that vines of the forest intuitively know where to grow in order to climb up to catch a patch of blue. Yet, which came first—the climbing vines that serve as a source of food, or the birds themselves that dropped the seeds from whence the vines came? In either case, season after season, they sprout and grow and climb to the top of the cabbage tree's tent-like umbrella of waving fans. While ways of the forest are secrets well-kept, it is evident that the sabal palm's network of crisscrossed steps is an ideal sort of trellis arrangement for vining flora. Grape vines, woodbine, trumpet creeper, honeysuckle, cross vine, hempweed, morning glory, moon vine and others happily climb this tree of life. While they compete for space, they seem to be comfortably compatible, and many species of vines can often be found on a single tree, their simultaneous blooms creating a delightful kaleidoscope of color. And when the flowers have faded, Mother Nature turns the vines' fall foliage as brilliant as any blossoms. The gleaming gold grapevine leaves and the resplendent red Virginia creeper reach out in all directions from the luminous green fronds to make the sabal palm appear as artistically decorated as any Christmas tree.

There is also an exquisite compatibility between the sabal's resident vines and birds, which find food and shelter among their tangled foliage. Cardinals most often choose twiggy, pocket-like places for their nests, while mockingbirds are more brave, usually perching their nests slightly more in the open, but on solid surfaces. These birds very often build a nest with one side solidly tucked up against the trunk of the tree or a limb. Doves are partial to the shelter of vine-covered cabbage palms as well, but they prefer a location closer to the ground than many other birds, constructing their nests only a few fronds up from the base of the trunk.

The flowers of trumpet creeper, cross vine, morning glory and honeysuckle provide nectar for hummingbirds, while seeds of woodbine and the fruit of grapevines provide food for other birds, as well as for raccoons, squirrels and similar creatures of the woodlands.

In addition to offering so many fine building sites, the *Sabal palmetto* is a well-stocked warehouse of construction materials for many creatures of the wild.

The strong, hair-like membranes that encase the trunk of most sabal palms prior to the time of the boot-drop resemble long, matted strands of ungraded steel wool, and have about as many uses.

Squirrels covet them for the construction of their tree house nests. The long, sturdy fibers are dry, yet remarkably resilient and easy to weave into intricate patterns. The weaving of such nests is probably easier than the extrication of the fibers used in the process. It is not unusual to see a squirrel laboriously tugging at the stringy fibers to pull them from the trunk, then carefully stuffing the material into his mouth until it will hold no more and he seems to have a golf ball in each cheek, then transporting it to the nest site.

Many birds also choose the cabbage tree's thread-like casing for the basic component in their house-building. Even the tiny hummingbird can extract with amazing speed the thinnest of the "hairs" for its thimble-size nest. These fibers are an excellent chinking material, as well as insulation for various human projects, including the old-fashioned practice of thickly lining a hole in the earth in which to store vegetables and fruits for safekeeping from cold or heat; the fluctuation of temperature from season to season in such dug-out larders was remarkably slight.

This fibrous material, though by no stretch of the imagination soft, was used extensively for stuffing mattress pads and pillows and lining baskets for eggs and other fragile items such as glass and china in many areas of the South.

In the years prior to the sloughing of the boots, it is not uncommon to see dozens of species of ferns, vines, wildflowers, weeds, mosses, lichens and even seedling trees, growing and thriving in the protected pockets between the base of the boot and the trunk. *Sabal palmetto* is also a hospitable host to many orchids, bromeliads, ficus, clusia and other species.

Often beginning its life as an epiphyte, the native strangler fig (*Ficus aurea*) can easily engulf a sabal and often does so rather rapidly. To the unaccustomed eye, a towering tree with both large, thick, leathery dark green leaves as well as big shining fronds and airborne roots reaching from several feet up the trunk down into the soil at the base of the tree, is a puzzling sight indeed. However, upon close inspection, it is easy to see that *Ficus aurea* has done its work and is making every effort to throttle its host—thus the name strangler fig.

Many other trees occasionally use the sabal palm as a nursery. In a clearing near Alva in Lee County, Florida, there is a four-foot wax myrtle, estimated to be at least a dozen years old, growing in a sabal boot four feet from the ground. Acorns of oaks, as well as seeds of maples, pines and other forest trees, often find all they need for germination in the warm, moist pockets, and they grow rather well for several years, but seldom longer, as their nutrition and water needs are more than can be supplied by the boot of a palm.

Plants that grow at the base of the boots are well supplied with rich growing material—humus from the natural decomposition process of bark and leaf shedding, plus natural fertilizer from bird and small animal droppings. It is a superbly efficient and dependable system.

The boots also serve as little vessels to hold rainwater and dew, from which woodland creatures drink. Some wrens and shrikes often build their nests among the fronds and can be seen splashing and preening in the little pools in the bottoms of the boots—quite a handy arrangement, since their bathing facilities and homesites are close to each other.

Other small birds—kinglets, wood pewees, flycatchers, blue-gray gnatcatchers and hummingbirds have been observed bathing in little crevices in the fronds. Even a tablespoonful of water is ample for the bath of a tiny bird.

The eagle-like caracaras seek out the strong fronds at the heads of sabal palms in which to build their nests, as do other large birds such as hawks and crows, which are afforded natural protection by the stairsteps of fronds that almost completely camouflage the nest from eyes below.

When the *Sabal palmetto's* fronds dehydrate completely, they at last part company with the tree. It is the leaf stem that actually breaks away, usually a foot or so from the trunk. In the natural state of the forest, these dry fronds simply fall in layers around the base of the tree.

When green, the leaf spine of the frond is stiff and strong; however, when completely dry, it breaks off easily. The fan part of the frond, extending out from the spine, becomes so brittle that even small animals walking over it break the dried fiber into small crumbles. Unlike many hardwood leaves of the forest that can take years to decompose, the crumbled fans of cabbage palms quickly return as humus to the soil.

The cabbage tree's usefulness does not cease with its death—while still standing, the dead trunks become perforated with the holes of cavity-nesters such as woodpeckers and flickers. And when the trunk does fall over, its service continues, as small animals—raccoons, rabbits, opossums and the like—find suitable quarters there for many years. Even when the decomposing trunk has sunk partially into the forest floor and is carpeted with a blanket of moss, small creatures burrow their way into the protected recesses of the trunk, where their young are out of sight and well-sheltered from the weather.

Finally, when the fallen trunks have completely given way, the decomposed matter is slowly incorporated into the forest floor by the microorganisms that live there and provide nutrients from which the next generation of trees will be nourished. Thus, the cycle of life and death and life again continues.

PART II

CHAPTER THREE

FROM CURRY COMBS TO COUNTRY HOMES

The many uses of the sabal palm

People, along with myriad other animals and plants, have found many ways to use and enjoy the sabal palm. Its small black berries which hang from stalks almost as big as the leaves are a stable food for raccoons, wild turkey, gray squirrels and many other species. People can eat them too. Writes biologist Richard Workman in *Growing Native*: "The flavor of sabal berries is pleasant. . . somewhat like a date. [But] since the berry is mostly seed, you have to eat a lot to get anything." Native American groups in Florida made a molasses-like syrup from the berries which was said to be not only tasty, but also highly nourishing.

The dish known as swamp cabbage comes from the tree's bud, which contains its embryonic leaves. This is the heart of the palm, and removing it kills the tree. A growing number of people think that eating one of the region's most honored trees is wasteful and inappropriate and should be declared unlawful. For those who find it difficult to restrain their appetites for heart of palm, it's interesting to note that there is an alternative delicacy reported to be of superior flavor. It is the heart of *Serenoa repens,* the saw palmetto, Florida's most abundant palm. Since the saw palmetto grows multiple arms or trunks, the harvesting of the bud does not necessarily kill the entire plant.

There was a time when work and dress hats for men and women were woven of cabbage palm frond strips. This craft is all but gone today, and survives mostly in some of the region's Native American communities. Seminole Indians say that when a cabbage palm grows in "happy ground," it will produce one new leaf every moon, thus fronds can be gathered throughout the year without harm to the palm. (In Puerto Rico, where the climate favors the wearing of hats, *Sabal palmetto* is commonly—albeit incorrectly—known as Puerto Rican hat palm. Although the hat palm *is* a relative of the sabal palm, it is a different species: *Sabal causiarum.*)

Woven table mats, baskets, trays, tote bags, and toys made from strips of sabal fronds still can be found at some isolated rural stores. Braided strips of cabbage fronds are remarkably strong and pliable, and many old-timers use them for numerous everyday tasks. It's said that in days of yore, without a cabbage frond mosquito whisk, Florida summers were all but intolerable.

There was a time, too, when the palm's fibrous trunk was made commercially into brooms and scrub brushes. Cedar Key, on Florida's west coast, was one of the chief manufacturing centers until plastics wiped out the demand for palm fiber brushes and brooms. As recently as 25 years ago, the sabal palm's trunk was made into large roller brushes and used by road contractors. Oliver Murray, an agri-businessman from Florida's rural Hendry County says the brushes made from sabal trunks were stronger, swept better and lasted three times longer than any others. And some horse-owners still favor home-made cabbage palm trunk curry combs over store-bought models.

Sabal palm trunks can make excellent plant

stands and containers when hollowed out enough to accommodate a plant's root system. Florida's wild ferns seem particularly to take to cabbage palm containers. Hollowed-out trunks are also used as holders for brooms and long-handled tools. When asked the age of one such holder in the kitchen of a cattle ranch in Florida's rural Glades County, the lady of the house replied, "Why, I ain't got no idea how old that thing is. Old as the house I reckon. It's been a-sittin' right there in that corner since 'fore I can remember."

While there are a good number of towns in the South that have the word *palm* in their names, none seems more aptly named than Palmdale, in south central Florida. In the early 1900s when Palmdale first came into being, there were tremendous hammocks of cabbage palms, and long, wide bands of them ran through the forests and fields, clearly indicating where water had washed the sabal seeds and where animals had added to the plantings. Now, almost 100 years later, the cabbage palm still grows widely throughout the area, but according to several old-timers "they ain't here nothin' like they usta be."

There are no fewer than three full-time sabal palm nurseries in Palmdale, and many specialists in the relocation of the cabbage palm.

In pioneer days, cabbage tree trunks, virtually immune to destruction by marine worms, were harvested extensively in Palmdale for use as dock pilings. Readily available with consistent thicknesses in lengths up to 60-70 feet and no branches to contend with, they were easy to install. Their longevity depended upon where and how they were used. And even today, Palmdale-grown cabbage palm fronds are still used for thatch roofs of walkways, sheds and chickees. The installation of fronds for such roofs is said to be more of an art than a science, and when they are installed correctly—as the Indians do—they last for years.

As to the durability of the sabal palm's trunk as a home-building material, one Palmdale family swears by its worth.

Tom Gaskins is best-known for his love of

cypress knees, knobby growths from the trees' roots, to which he dedicated a museum. "I'm sure I'm the only fellow in the world who's shown cypress knees on Johnny Carson's *Tonight Show* not just once, but twice!" he says.

But when it was time to build a house, Gaskins chose not cypress, but sabal palm logs. How did he do it? "It's real simple," Gaskins replies. "First, choose trees with trunks the same thickness as nearly as possible. Then bore a hole all the way through the trunk vertically and pour creosote through it. Situate the trunks vertically on a sill to which they're nailed. This is just like any other house construction. And, of course, they're nailed to a two-by-four around the top. Basically, that's it! It's a round construction—keeps heat and cold out, and you can forget maintenance—there is none."

The house has been standing for more than 20 years and remains in good shape; Gaskins' son, Tom, Jr. and his wife, Billie Jo, live in it now, although he admits that its construction took a bit more work than his Dad likes to admit.

"At first, we considered building the house stockade style, and actually planting or placing ends of the logs in the ground. But it didn't take long to figure out that this was not a wise plan. Even when treated with creosote, a sawed-off raw end when stuck or planted in the ground, is going to deteriorate," Tom, Jr. explains.

"I did not want any part of this log house building to be anything but the best we could make it, so I showed the plans to a friend of mine, a civil engineer, in Jacksonville. It was his opinion that the plans [and] specifications were viable—that the structure would be strong and long-lived."

In order to have an eight-foot ceiling, the logs were cut nine feet long and notched to sit on the sill and at the same time lap over the outside of the sill.

"There are 276 logs situated side-by-side in the perimeter of this house," Tom, Jr. says, recalling that one of the most time-consuming and difficult tasks was finding the right logs.

"We knew, of course, that the trees [that would become the logs] had to be straight, and ideally they should be the same size.

"We knew we'd have to find a place with a whole lot of trees so we could select the ones that would fit the plan of the house. The best place I knew was Boar Hammock, which is owned by Mr. and Mrs. James H. Dilley. James was the Clerk of Court of Glades County at that time, and a real good friend. Well, when I told him why we wanted the trees, he said, 'Good. I'll give them to you.' And that's what he did."

Once cut, the logs were loaded 12 at a time crossways on the back of a truck. "It was all two men could do to shoulder and carry out a nine-foot green section of a cabbage palm from that hammock. It was back-breaking, but we kept at it until we had enough to build the house."

Boring the first hole took a lot of experimenting and trial and error. "But we finally got the first one bored. My Dad was in the hospital at that time so I sent him a card with one line on it: THE FIRST LOG IS BORED!"

And, as it turned out, that first log was not used in the house. Instead, it's used as a "show and tell" memento for people who want to know about building a sabal palm log house.

Father and son poured creosote down the holes, however both agreed later that it was not necessary. "The important thing," says Tom, Jr., "was that the ends of the logs be kept absolutely clear of the ground, and, that the logs be turned opposite as to their natural way of growth. We found this out by sheer luck. A friend from Miami, Mac McAlhaney, suggested that we turn them upside down so the natural stickers of the palm's bark, or skin, would help shed water." When the sabal palm's boots rot away as the tree grows taller, a rough spiny texture is left and the bark is generally not smooth. Nature utilizes this system to catch water for the benefit of the tree while it's growing. However, by reversing the direction in house-building for humans, this system can be used to help the house shed water, which is of paramount importance, says Tom, Jr. "Whenever a log or board, including cabbage logs, has a place that holds moisture—even a small place—germs develop and rot will follow. You can count on it. Therefore, a cabbage log cabin or house built by situating the logs horizontally, in my opinion, would not last long, simply because there would be so many places that moisture could gather. After a heavy rain, I've noticed many times that the sides of my house are dry."

And how long did the construction of a cabbage palm log house take? Tom, Jr. smiles.

"The longest, hardest 11 months of my life!"

CHAPTER FOUR

INDIGENOUS ARCHITECTURE

The art of the chickee

Following the ancient patterns of their ancestors, the Seminole Indians' chickee is a work of rustic art, remarkably suited for life in a subtropical climate. Yet, the exact origin of chickees is lost in antiquity. Records do show, however, that Florida Indians have for centuries built and lived in shelters constructed of materials from the sabal palm and peeled green cypress trees, the latter being generally used for the pole framework.

When a chickee is built in a hammock under the canopy of trees, there is nothing about its structure to jar or conflict with natural surroundings. It seems to be a part of the hammock itself, blending into the natural forest tapestry. There was a measure of safety in this characteristic as well, since chickees are not easily spotted from afar.

This camouflaging is not happenstance, but an integral part of the Indians' plan. Even the positioning of fronds on the rafters approximate the appearance of dead fronds on palm trees. And the coloration of the fronds, from the day of installation to the weather-cured color they become when aged, harmonizes with the natural forest tones. Fronds in a chickee roof are virtually the same color as fronds that are naturally sloughed by cabbage trees year after year.

It was also extremely important that the inhabitants be able to see from all sides in case of danger from any enemy—man or beast.

Close inspection of a chickee built by Indians specifically for their own habitation clearly demonstrates why they are constructed as they are. From the beginning, common sense dictated that the chickee should be situated to take advantage of prevailing winds, nature's air conditioning.

Typically, chickees were 8 to 10 feet by 14 to 16 feet and open on all sides. If a longer building was needed, this was accomplished by adding vertical pole supports to elongate the living space.

The floor of the chickee, again for practical reasons, always was built well above the forest floor. One of those reasons was to allow enough space underneath the floor for "critters" to crawl without being too tempted to come in uninvited. Seasonal high waters flowed under the structure and not over the floor, and air circulation below the floor helped minimize the dankness of the earth. The frond roof provided its own constant ventilation—albeit subtle—between the blades of the fronds.

Thatch is not only considered the oldest form of roofing, thatching is thought to be one of the oldest methods of building dwellings as well. Anthropologists say early Southern Indians made wigwam-like structures and covered them by snugging the frond-thatch from the ground to the building's rounded top, which was always taller in the middle, and usually high enough for an adult to stand in. The shape typically resembled a Quonset hut. These structures had few or no windows, but did occasionally have a small, narrow slit at one end, through which residents could see outside. Such openings could easily be covered by simply inserting a frond or two across the slit.

The wide overhangs (two or three feet all

around) also served another purpose, that of allowing the soft, morning sun as well as late afternoon sunlight into the structure. And the high ceiling helped protect the interior from the searing sun's peak heat at midday.

Often, on the windward side of the home, particularly if that side was relatively unprotected by trees, a lean-to roof extension almost to the ground was built for further protection from high winds and inundating rains.

Some students of history, particularly those interested in the deep South and its early architecture, believe that the wide overhangs of old Florida style houses are simply an outgrowth of the Seminole chickee overhang.

Heavy layers of fronds dry to a silvery bronze color that very effectively reflects sunlight. Although a palm thatch roof repels rain, minute spaces between the fronds allow rising hot air within the chickee to escape.

On a bright, sunlit day in mid-July, Seminole Tribal Councilman Jack Smith sits quietly in a chickee on the playground of the Brighton Reservation in Glades County, Florida. There are no trees nearby—nothing to provide shade. Yet, it is pleasantly cool beneath the sabal palm frond roof. And, with all sides being open, there is a light breeze blowing through. Smith is talking about chickees. "There are quite a few here who make their living with the tree—the cabbage tree—building chickees on contract. They go all over, not just Florida but to many different places.

"People who want them built come here, or phone or write, (Seminole Tribe of Florida, Brighton Reservation, Route 6, Box 668, Okeechobee, FL 34974, 941-763-4128.) They hear about chickees from others who have them. The materials they take from here, the reservation. These are not companies, these are individuals who have learned the way of building chickees from their elders who learned from their elders. It is a craft that has been handed down from father to son for centuries."

Smith is a large, broad-shouldered man,

quiet and unassuming. He speaks softly, using as few words as he can to explain. "When chickees are built properly, they will last 10 to 15 years. It all depends on the individual who is building it and how he builds it."

The materials that go into the construction of a chickee are all indigenous. But although they once were readily available over much of Florida, sabal palms and cypress trees are becoming scarce in some areas.

"We have to cut cypress for chickees from the reservation. We are no longer allowed to cut cypress from other land. The fronds from the cabbage tree, we cut from our trees here. From one tree, we will cut only a few of the lowest rings or rounds, then we go to another and do the same. This does not harm the tree," Smith says, adding that not many years ago, there were so many palms and so many cypress trees that no one ever thought there would ever be a shortage.

In fact, in the not-so-distant past, many people took a very dim view of sabal palms, and thought nothing of destroying vast numbers of them. In his 1963 book, *Florida Facts and Fallacies,* Tom Gaskins wrote: "I cut 105 cabbages in one day for 65 cents each. Frank Jones cut 305 in one day to feed his hogs. . . . In [some Florida counties] they are such a nuisance that cattlemen hire crews to kill them by pouring kerosene in the buds."

But Larry Lucky, the tax appraiser of Glades County, Florida, thinks it's time to stop squandering the cabbage palm. Because Lucky's profession requires him to crisscross the region regularly, he's able to keep a close eye on agricultural and business trends.

He estimates that at least 150 sabal palms are trucked out of Glades County every day. "These trees need to be saved. They need to be re-planted and," he says, "many of them are." But others are simply cut out and discarded when land is cleared. And that's what bothers Lucky.

"The effort needs to be made to save every cabbage palm possible. They are links in the chain of our ecosystem that can not be replaced."

CHAPTER FIVE

QUICK COMFORT

How to make a sabal palm lean-to

In days gone by, there were countless people, both Native Americans and European settlers, who trekked for days across the lower South's vast forests, prairies, scrub and piney woods for various reasons: hunting, fishing, going to a distant settlement, or seeking a new home. These traveling people often found themselves deep in the woods for days and nights at a time. They needed to know how to survive—and do it comfortably, if at all possible.

One of the most important things to know how to do was to fashion lean-to sleeping quarters from available materials.

Wanderin' Wind, a Florida Seminole with life-long knowledge of the wild, speaks from considerable experience. He says that ideally, it was good to find a couple of sapling oaks or other hardwood trees growing several feet apart. "It all depends," he explains, "on how and where the trees are growing and how long you want the lean-to to be. Then, if you happen to have a rope with you, lace it across from tree to tree. If there's no rope available, scour the forest for vines—grapevines, moonflower vines, honeysuckle, woodbine, smilax or any others, except, of course, poison ivy, which you want to stay far away from. If the vines are thin or weak, twist two or three together, or plait three vines together, which will give added strength. In the absence of a rope, lace the vines back and forth from tree to tree.

"After you've done this, cut a number of cabbage [palm] fronds, leaving the stalk long. Cut the end of the stalk in a sharp point. Thrust the pointed ends securely in the ground in a row between the two trees. Then insert a frond fan downward through the upright fan that's been stuck in the ground, so that they interlace. Repeat until the thatching is as high as needed.

"The more fronds used and the more skillfully the fronds are inserted into each other, the tighter the structure will be, thus keeping out both wind and water."

Wanderin' Wind says that on occasions when hunters anticipated being in the woods over a rather long period of time, two thatched lean-tos would be built slanting toward each other in an "A" shape. Depending upon how carefully they were constructed, the structures would often last a year or more, and some hunters would go back to the same ones from time to time.

As the Indians knew, not only do such lean-to structures serve to keep a person dry and out of the wind, they are not highly visible. Being built of forest materials they naturally blended into the woodland landscape.

For sleeping, a pallet can be made by placing layers of cabbage palm fronds flat on the forest floor, then piling and packing pine needles on top of the fronds, which makes a surprisingly comfortable forest bed. Wanderin' Wind says he knows those materials might seem unlikely, but, he promises, "If you've ever slept direct on the ground, and then sleep on a palm and pine needle bed, you'll say there's a whole heap of difference."

Cayo Costa Isle #3
Clyde Butcher

31

SEVEN CABBAGE CUT
32   CLYDE BUTCHER

Chassahowitzka River #2
Clyde Butcher

MISTY HAMMOCK
CLYDE BUTCHER

THE SABAL PALM
IN FULL BLOOM.
Luther Oehlbeck

HUMMINGBIRD
NEST BUILT WITH
SABAL PALM
FIBER.
Luther Oehlbeck

38

SABALS AND WILDFLOWERS, JUST WEST OF LAKE OKEECHOBEE, FLORIDA.

LUTHER OEHLBECK

SABALS AT SUN-
SET, GLADES
COUNTY,
FLORIDA.

C.C. F. GACHET

THE GASKINS HOUSE IN
PALMDALE, FLORIDA
MADE OF SABAL PALM
LOGS.

LUTHER OEHLBECK

GOSSAMER THREADS THAT "PEEL" OFF THE
EDGES OF FROND BLADES.

LUTHER OEHLBECK

TOM GASKINS, JR. DEMONSTRATES THE USE OF AN
AUGER ON SABAL PALM LOGS BEFORE FILLING THEM
WITH CREOSOTE.

LUTHER OEHLBECK

CHICKEE

LUTHER OEHLBECK

COILED SABAL PALM FROND BASKET.

ROBIN BROWN, COURTESY DAVID MEO

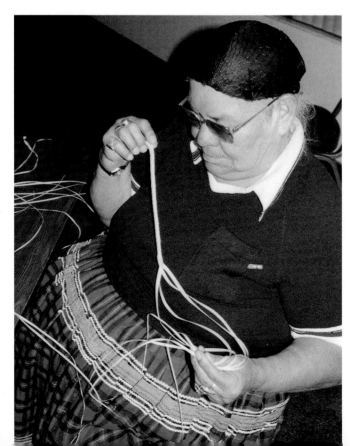

A FLORIDA
SEMINOLE
WOMAN MAK-
ING SABAL
PALM ROPE.

LUTHER

OEHLBECK

THE UNDERSIDE OF A SABAL-THATCHED CHICKEE.

LUTHER OEHLBECK

Sometimes Mother Nature throws the cabbage palm a curve.

Luther Oehlbeck

SABAL PALM FLUTTER MILL

In Marjorie Kinnan Rawlings' classic novel, *The Yearling*, Jody built himself a palm frond flutter mill that remains fascinating to those who have read about or seen simple forest materials made into a little moving mill-wheel.

To make a flutter-mill, you will need: clippers or a pocket knife, two or three strips of palm frond (two strips will make four arms; three will yield six arms) two forked twigs about a foot long and one small, straight

DRAWING BY ANNE FRIEDMAN

BRANCH FOR A CROSSBAR. IN THE BOOK, JODY MADE SURE THAT THE TWIG HE CUT FOR THE CROSSBAR WAS ABOUT THE SIZE OF A PENCIL—AND STRAIGHT, ROUND AND SMOOTH.

ASSEMBLY IS SIMPLE: CUT THE STRIPS OF PALM FROND ABOUT TEN TO 12 INCHES LONG, WHICH WILL MAKE THE ARMS OF THE FLUTTER-MILL FIVE OR SIX INCHES LONG. (JODY MADE A TINY WHEEL, WITH STRIPS ONLY FOUR INCHES LONG.) IN THE CENTER OF EACH STRIP, CAREFULLY CUT A LENGTHWISE SLIT JUST BIG ENOUGH TO RECEIVE THE INSERTED CROSS-BAR BRANCH. GENTLY RUN THE CROSSBAR THROUGH THE SLITS. LIKE THE ARMS OF A WINDMILL, THE PALM STRIPS MUST BE AT ANGLES.

PLACE THE Y-SHAPED TWIGS A LITTLE CLOSER TOGETHER THAN THE CROSSBAR BRANCH, PUSHING THEM FIRMLY INTO THE EDGE OF A STREAM OR A POND OR EVEN IN THE GROUND, IN WHICH CASE A HOSE CAN BE USED. PLACE THE CROSSBAR WITH ITS FROND ARMS ACROSS THE YS OF THE TWIGS. THE ARMS OF THE FLUTTER-MILL WHEEL SHOULD JUST TOUCH THE SURFACE OF THE WATER; IF YOU'RE USING A HOSE, THE FROND WHEEL SHOULD CLEAR THE GROUND A FEW INCHES.

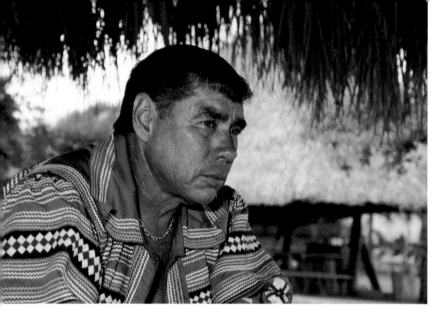

JAMES BILLIE, CHIEF
OF THE SEMINOLE
TRIBE OF FLORIDA.
LUTHER OEHLBECK

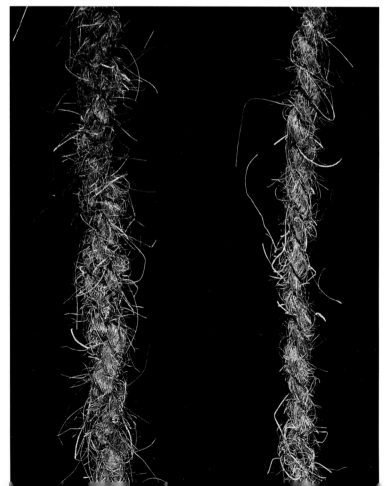

WE KNOW VERY LITTLE ABOUT THE USES
OF FIBERS BY FLORIDA'S FIRST PEOPLE
BECAUSE ROPE, TWINE, AND FABRIC
RARELY SURVIVE THE PASSAGE OF YEARS.
YET, FROM THE MANGROVE PEAT OF
MARCO ISLAND ON THE SOUTHWEST
COAST OF FLORIDA HAVE COME FRAG-
MENTS OF NETS, LINES, AND ROPES USED
BY A SOPHISTICATED CULTURE SKILLED IN
FISHING. IN BOTH INSTANCES, THE BASIC
FIBERS SEEM BE TO FROM PALMS. THIS IS
A REPLICATION OF WHAT THEIR PALM
CORD MAY HAVE LOOKED LIKE.
ROBIN BROWN

44

SABALS BY THE CALOOSAHATCHEE. Luther Oehlbeck

FLORIDA IS THE LAND OF PALMS... FORESTS OF PALMS BESIDE OUR STREAMS AND LAKES! THICKETS OF PALMS IN OUR WOODS! THE WORD "PALM" STANDS FOR ALL THAT IS NOBLE AND GRAND IN THE PLANT WORLD.
Dr. Henry Nehrling, 1933

COMMON FLICKER AT THE
"DOOR" OF HIS CABBAGE
TREE HOME. KENT JAGER

FLORIDA STATE SEAL
IN 1970, ANOTHER HONOR
WAS BESTOWED UPON
SABAL PALMETTO, WHEN IT
WAS NAMED TO REPLACE
THE COCONUT PALM ON
THE STATE SEAL OF
FLORIDA.

SABALS ALONG FLORIDA'S ORANGE RIVER.
BARBARA OEHLBECK

CARDINAL'S NEST AT THE LYKES FIRE TOWER IN MUSE,
FLORIDA. MANY BIRDS LIVING NEAR CABBAGE PALMS
FIND THE GOSSAMER THREADS THAT PEEL FROM THE
FRONDS UNPARALLELED AS A NEST-LINING MATERIAL.
THEY ARE SMOOTH, YET STRONG, AND WICK AWAY
MOISTURE, WHICH ALLOWS THE CENTER OF THE NEST
TO STAY DRY AND INTACT.
C.C.F. GACHET

CHAPTER SIX

BOONDOGGLING AND BASKETRY

Cabbage palm crafts

Although a dictionary defines boondoggling as doing unnecessary, wasteful and counterproductive work, Native Americans will tell you that it's an amusingly elaborate craft, one passed down from woman to woman as a way to entertain children and each other. Using strips of palm fronds, Indian women create finely woven, multi-chambered little objects. Some look like rattlesnake tails, others are intricate chains, some take the shape of flowers or animals and still others can trap unwary fingers.

The craft goes back further than anyone now living can remember, although a century or so ago it was probably not known by this name. And even the venerable ones well along into what some Indians refer to as "setting sun time" say it is an art that's been handed down orally and by demonstration from *hoke-tee-li-tee* (old woman) to *hoke-tee-ti-mit-nit-ti-tee* (young woman) with no written or drawn instructions.

A skilled *Sabal palmetto* boondoggling artist sitting comfortably under a chickee creating her pieces can lead the onlooker to believe that this is not a difficult task at all, simply an easy pastime. But a closer look shows that every move of her hands is deft indeed, as she weaves long, straight frond blades into a flowery mandala, a sturdy basket or a length of cord. The Indians' four-plait cord—as opposed to the common three-strand braid that yields a somewhat fat but flat cord—is perfectly round, with a herringbone pattern. It is a very strong, long-lasting weave.

Pieces of boondoggling last for years. The frond blades dry naturally without wrinkling. At first, the dried color is a soft lichen shade of gray-green. As the fronds continue to naturally cure, the Indians say the blades become the color of *chum-pee* (honey). If they become discolored by dust, the pieces can be washed with a soft spray of water, shaken gently, then hung to dry in the light.

Boondoggling is sometimes demonstrated at large craft shows, where pieces are also offered for sale. While boondoggling is not by any means a lost or fading art, it is certainly one that is not commonplace.

A Seminole mother was busy weaving, while her small daughter stood pressed next to her, looking intently at her mother's fingers as they nimbly tugged and teased the fronds into the shape of a basket. Asked, "How old will your daughter be before she learns how to weave as you do?" the mother replied without looking up or pausing, "She was born knowing how."

There is a long tradition of palm frond basketry among the indigenous peoples of the South. Most of their cabbage palm baskets, however, were not decorative; they were generally used for gathering or storing food. These days, though, Indian basketry is classed as "collectable" and is becoming increasingly sought-after and popular with mainstream America.

The most widely used sabal palm basket was

shallow and tray-like. Also called a winnowing basket, it could be used to sift corn and other grains. There were two types of winnowing baskets—one made with a solidly woven bottom, the other with an open weave that facilitated sifting. The rather small "berry basket" was just that: a very lightweight basket for berry-picking, sometimes with a plaited handle long enough to be carried loosely over the arm. The bases of these baskets were usually quite firm and square, and the basket itself was at least as deep as it was wide, and sometimes deeper. Frequently, pickers lined the bottom of their berry baskets with small pieces of freshly cut fronds to protect the inside of the basket from wet or crushed fruit.

Pack baskets were the largest and strongest of the cabbage palm frond baskets. Made with a slightly flared rim at the top, pack baskets were usually from 24 to 30 inches deep, with a fairly square bottom. Occasionally, long plaited cords were attached for back carrying. People used these big, sturdy baskets for heavy objects; they were also used to load beasts of burden. Dry waste and work materials such as fabric and thread also were stored in pack baskets.

The smallest cabbage palm basket is called a medicine bag, in which herbs, beads, and other little ceremonial objects could be safely carried. Envelope-shaped and tightly woven with a remarkable herringbone pattern, these baskets were often used for other small items as well.

PART III

CHAPTER SEVEN

A VERY HOLY TREE

Chief Billie on the sabal palm

There is probably no one living today who knows the sabal palm's characteristics, uses, and worth more thoroughly than the Chief of the Seminole Tribe of Florida, James Billie, nor anyone who holds the state tree in higher esteem. In fact, *Sabal palmetto* was honored by Florida's Indians long before the Land of Flowers was populated with Europeans, and that reverence continues.

For untold generations, the sabal palm has played a vital role in the lives of the Seminoles and other indigenous people of the lower South, as well as the other tribes before them. The tree's essential role persists today, as does its honored status.

"The cabbage tree to us Seminoles, Miccosukees [and] Muscogees is the *Shee-lah-mah-shee-kee Tahl-cho-bee.* We make our shelters from it. It provides food for us. It is our protector." Sitting in a chickee at the Big

Cypress Reservation, Chief Billie tries to find English words adequate to express the tree's rich meaning. *"Tahl-cho-bee nock-hoon-lee. . . It is sacred. . . a very holy tree. . . . It protects us. . . . Its many parts protect us from the burning sun, from the rain that would ruin our living areas, from the winds that would whip and beat us down and from winter's cold.*

"The cabbage palm is a primary source of food from the land," Chief Billie says. "We don't plant it. Water plants it by washing the seeds to various areas. The wind plants it. It's the way of wind to blow seeds around, and animals and birds plant it year after year. It's the seed and grain feeders mainly—raccoons, 'possums, and bears, along with mocking-birds, robins, blue jays, scrub jays and some others."

Unlike those who were to come later, the Indians made use of virtually every part of *Sabal palmetto*. When a tree was cut for logs with which to build, the fronds were used for thatching the roof, the bud of the palm was the next meal, and when bread was in short supply, the Indians had a method of beating the palm fronds to produce a flour-like meal from which they made bread. They even extracted salt from the palm by leaching, or running water slowly through ashes of burned trunks and boiling down the solution—something like the method used to make potash.

"And the berries," Chief Billie explains, "we grind them into a soft pulp that makes them into something like peanut butter. Then we dip this in grease. It's a good taste—a solid food and good for you. If we don't have grease, we eat it without.

"Spoons and forks are cut from the spine of the fronds, and long ladles for stirring. They last a long time, but when they do wear out, we just cut a fresh frond and make new ones."

Even then, however, he says the worn out utensils are not rendered useless—they are either added to the cooking fires, or returned to the earth as mulch.

He goes on: "The heart of the cabbage palm is sweet and tender. When a hunter is on the run in the woods, he can feed on raw heart of the palm and never get hungry." Chief Billie smiles, adding, "The cabbage heart has a lot of strength in it but almost zero calories. Of course, it's good cooked, too, but it's even better for you when it's fresh and raw. Ask any bear!" He laughs. "Bears—like humans—love the cabbage tree heart!

"And," he adds, "the seeds of the cabbage palm play an important role in our ritual dances. Dried seeds make music for keeping the rhythm. When they are completely dry, they are very hard. Then we put them in shakers, which are gourds, coconut shells and shelled out dried buckskin. The sounds have different pitches when they are in different shakers."

He explains that the soft base of the tree's heart is an excellent food for hogs—and that children like it too, but for a different reason:

"When children play in the woods, they often tie pieces of the heart base onto their feet. They're soft and cool and feel good on your feet, but they don't last long. It's a game—sort of a toy—just to see how long they will stay on your feet.

"Another children's game is 'ride the horses.' Well, the horses are palm fronds. A young boy straddles the spine, holding tight onto the neck where it's cut from the tree. The fan-leaf, which is the horse's tail, is, of course, back of the boy's legs. Sometimes we'd trim the 'tail' into different shapes. . . .

"We'd run so fast on those horses, I mean really fast! Racing through the woods, skidding around trees and corners, jumping across creeks and runs and falling in sometimes, too! And always we'd be kicking. . . just like we'd see horses kick."

Laughing at his boyhood memories, Chief Billie says, "I'd ride for hours. It's a good, clean game. . . gives boys exercise outdoors in fresh air and sunshine. And, it teaches them to use what they have."

While the use of sabal palm as a shelter material is well-known, few have the knowledge that Chief James Billie does. In fact, he built the two largest sabal palm chickees in the United States. The biggest, approximately 100' x 50' is on the Tampa Indian Reservation near *Coo-taun-chobee* (Big Shore Line), while the other, about 40' x 80' is on the Hollywood Indian Reservation at Native Village, Hollywood, Florida.

"It's *tahl-cho-bee,* the Seminole word meaning large stalk tree. We cut the largest trees to use as frame and corner posts to hold the roof. After the chickee is made, we make tables, stools. . . whatever we need, from the trunks.

"The roof is thatch. Cutting the fronds for the roof does not kill the tree. They are used liked shingles. One row sheds water to the next, [and] that one to the next row until the roof is done. For a large roof, it can take up to 10,000 fronds. But remember: the tree is *not* killed."

The trunks of cabbage palms served other purposes in the lives of the Indians. When split, they made fine troughs for various purposes, including channels or conduits to carry water above ground to wherever it was needed.

And, during some of the Indian wars, stout sabal palm trunks were widely used for building forts. Nothing absorbed or stopped bullets—even cannon balls—as well as the spongy wood of heavy *Sabal palmetto* trunks.

As Chief Billie continues to outline some of the many uses of the cabbage palm, he alternately smiles and becomes pensive, even sad. Yet frequently, there is his deep-throated chuckle.

"The trunks are fine for carvings, too: faces of humans, animals, signs, and other things." He says the Seminoles also prize *Sabal palmetto* for making weapons.

"The green leaf stalks make great bows and arrows. Our sons learn the bow-and-arrow art with these—to make them and to shoot them. We can make them quickly without spending money, but we also make some to sell. When the stalks are green, they will bend, yet they're very strong. The arrows are made of the stalks, too."

Chief Billie sits in silence, then adds, "It is

not the way of sons to speak out about their skills. But I will tell you: most of them become fine marksmen with the bow and arrow."

For a few moments he is quiet, then says, "And there are other things we make. Braided hats and baskets, vessels of various shapes and sizes to carry things in. We make all these from strips of the green fronds. They last a long time. We make them as we need them, to sell or to use ourselves."

Suddenly, he smiles broadly. "I have had some strange things happen to me—one time, I was going through the swamp when the water was high. It was hard to walk, pulling my feet out of the water and muck and trying to step over fallen limbs and stumps. I came to a cabbage palm that had partly fallen over, so I grabbed the trunk and started sliding under the head of it when, almost like lightning, something slid right by my head. A rattler! It had been in the head of the palm. Well, as that snake went one way, I made my way back!

"And I can tell this story, too. You can slip up a cabbage tree trunk OK, but don't try slid-ing down. I *still* have splinters in my backside to prove the point. The trunk of a cabbage palm is totally a spine-type, full of sharp splinters from the crown to the ground!

"Another hazard is this: the cabbage palm is a natural haven for wasps. It's their home — they'll fight for it. Best leave the palm alone when you see wasps around."

The sabal is even prized by Native American anglers: "If you want to catch a fish, just find yourself a cabbage tree. Listen for the squawks of tree frogs in the palms where they live. You'll be hearing the best bait you'll ever have for catching fish." Grinning, his eyes twinkling, he adds, "This is not very good for frogs but sure good for fishing!

"And a cabbage palm frond is a fine umbrella, but a tree is still better if you find yourself caught in the rain," says Chief Billie. "Just lean back against the trunk and watch the rain go by. You'll stay dry. A rain shower in the woods is a good time for dreaming when you're under the arms of a cabbage palm."

Although fire-starting is no longer much of a

problem for Seminoles, before matches, it was a complicated—and critically important—process. And the sabal palm was an important part, says Chief Billie.

"The fiber of the cabbage tree is greatly valuable for a number of uses, but none can match its value as a means to starting fire. Not may people today ever think of not having matches, but if you are ever without them, you might need to know how to get a fire going.

"It's a good thing to know that the fiber of the cabbage palm, when it is totally dry, as the layers under the biggest frond stems away from the weather are, is very flammable. A spark from any source, striking a piece of steel against flint, or rock against rock to make sparks will kindle a fire in the palm's dry fiber.

"We know that fire is a gift from the gods, but we know, too, that fire is friend or foe, so we always need to know how to start a fire—and how to put fire out! Each father teaches each son."

Not surprisingly, James Billie has a few good stories about the sabal palm.

"There is a tale, maybe a legend, that I've heard all my life about a skunk-ape. The tale goes that the skunk-ape roams through the forests and swamps leaving a long-lasting, foul-smelling path wherever he goes. But I've yet to talk to anyone who has actually seen him.

"Well, this story I'm about to tell is not a legend. This is true. It happened to me. I was flying low, in my little airplane, banking first one way, then another, looking all around.

"All of a sudden, I saw a tall swamp cabbage palm shaking violently. There was no wind at all. It was a very still morning and none of the other trees were even moving. Yet those big, wide fronds on that one tree were dancing up and down, back and forth in a dizzy frenzy. I took the plane as low as I could, just skimming the tree-tops, to get the closest look possible, when suddenly I thought: that's the skunk-ape eating the swamp cabbage.

"I banked around again and lowered the plane even more to just above the top of that big cabbage tree. Then I saw him! Those hand-paws were gouging every bite of that swamp cabbage heart out of the top of that palm. And then I saw that it wasn't the skunk-ape, it was a big bear. He was so big he was having a hard time balancing himself in the top of the tree as he dug out the heart of that palm."

He smiles. "Now, I'll tell one more story," he says with finality. "During one of the Indian wars, the military men were fighting in the swamps of south Florida during a long, hot summer, when a sudden storm broke and there was nowhere to go to get out of it. Well, the Indians didn't need to go anywhere, they were at home in the swamp.

"They just reached up, cut cabbage fronds to keep the rain off and kept going while the soldiers got drenched to the skin, including their heads and feet and all their gear. As the rain kept pouring, the soldiers saw that the Indians were undaunted, and in that swamp, they had every advantage over the soldiers. At that point, the soldiers turned in a hurry and retreated right out of that swamp! In less time

than it takes to tell, those soldiers learned that fighting men is one thing, but fighting the ominous elements of a swamp when you've never done it before is something else."

He holds up his hand, and his far-away expression returns. "This is not a story—this is truth—reality." His voice is low and resonant with emotion.

"When I have been away, and then return to the land, to the swamp, I find myself looking quickly from one direction to another. I think I am trying to see everything at once—all the things I've not seen while being away. When my eyes come to rest on the swamp cabbage tree with its tousled head held high and proud like a fine painting against the great blue sweep of the sky, I think about the small wild animals and birds that make their homes up in that head among the fronds, and in the crotches of the boots.

"I hear the plaintive windsong, and I hear the soft sounds of the fan-leafs brushing against each other. It is like a litany of the land. This is the. . . soul of my world. An overwhelming feeling of romance overtakes me. This is the *e-fer-caw* (heart) of my *in-like-e-taw* (heaven) on earth."

After a short silence, Chief Billie explains, "It's a fact that cabbage palm trees grow on ground that's a little higher than the surrounding area. It doesn't have to be much higher, just a slight mound or rise of a little sand ridge. I see such a ridge with the cabbage trees reaching straight up tall and proud toward the big sky, and I know I've found peace—and safety—in the swamp. This is my secret sanctuary."

With reverence, Chief James Billie and his people have for centuries nurtured nature's gift of *Sabal palmetto*. The cabbage palm is an integral part of their being, woven into the fibers of their lives, common to their shared existence. The Seminole's *isteameheilst*—love—for the cabbage tree is born of a profound respect, handed down from generation to generation.

Chief Billie sits silent and still. After a while, he lifts his eyes, looking far away upriver and says, "There is no exaggerating the evil of waste. For thousands of years, our people have lived off the country, the products of the land from within the depths of earth itself without despoiling or consuming it.

"Now, we have to ask: How long can the suicidal course of destroying the land and its gifts be pursued—and to what end?

"For all the generations of our people that have been, fathers and mothers have taught sons and daughters how to use what has been put there for us without wiping out and wasting.

"It has been our way for all the time that we have been."

CHAPTER EIGHT

LIFE WITH THE CABBAGE TREE

A Florida cracker remembers

"This was the best place on earth to be a boy, and it's the best place on earth to be a man, to be a rancher. Living with Florida natives—and I include plants as well as people—is healthy and soul-satisfying."

John Franklin Pearce is standing on the banks of the Kissimmee River on land originally owned by his Daddy, the same land where he spent his boyhood in northern Glades County that lies west of Florida's Lake Okeechobee. These are some of his memories of growing up there, and his reflections about the sabal palm's place in his life:

The native I think of most often is the cabbage tree. Of course, the right name for this tree is sabal palm, but we didn't know that when I was a young'n growing up in the Kissimmee River Valley. Back then, the cabbage palm was just called "cabbage."

The river marsh is bordered by cabbage and oak hammocks, usually determined by the high water mark of the river. There were some cab-

bage trees growing on high knolls in the river marsh and also along the banks of the river where the land was high enough to keep from flooding.

When I was a young boy my Dad owned more hogs than cows. The hogs would get fat on cabbage berries and acorns. The cabbage trees bloom once a year on a stem about five feet long, which comes from the head of the cabbage. When fully matured, the blossoms develop into berries, which are about the size of an English pea. The kernel is very hard and is eaten and scattered by birds, raccoons, and hogs.

We would hunt the hogs with dogs and usually the hogs would be in groups. We'd drive those hogs just like cattle, using the dogs to keep them bunched together. Hog wire holding pens were used to hold them in until we'd gathered all the fat barrow hogs in that area. While they were in the holding pen, we'd cut the cabbage berries and feed them to the hogs because there wasn't any store-bought feed.

One of my fondest recollections is Daddy and Mother taking all four of us children camping in the cabbage woods. Now, I'll have to explain where the cabbage woods are. It is probably the largest concentration of cabbage tree hammocks in the state of Florida. The Seminole Indian Reservation at Brighton—some 40,000 acres—is in the middle of this huge concentration of cabbage hammocks.

When our folks took us camping to the cabbage woods, it was usually at Christmas or Thanksgiving. We'd stretch a big tent and then cut cabbage fans to make a mattress. To make them lie level, we would split the fans. Over these fans, mother would spread quilts and blankets. Those cabbage fans placed right on the ground stacked to a height of about eight inches became our "Beautyrest."

[Indian leader] Billy Bowlegs had a camp on a high knoll in the middle of one of the big cabbage hammocks. I went by his camp with my Dad many times, and he was always glad to see us. His chickee was built of cabbage logs and roofed with cabbage fans. He had a garden of corn and pumpkin and some other vegetables.

He used cabbage logs to fence out the hogs. These logs were stacked and built just like the rail fences that the pioneers built. Billy always had a fire, which was kept burning by pushing up the cabbage logs that were positioned in the form of a star.

Some Indians buried their dead in cabbage log pens. My Dad said he came upon one that had a skeleton and a few meager belongings that included pots and bowls.

During the Great Depression, the land reverted to the state or was acquired by a few big land companies. About 1938, the Florida Legislature passed the Murphy Act, which gave anyone the right to acquire state land by paying a portion of the back taxes. This started a land boom in Florida that meant the end of the free range. My Dad bought some of this land that bordered the cabbage woods, which consisted mostly of Kissimmee River marsh land. There were a few cabbage trees on its western border. One of the old-timers who had squatted on the lakefront also had several hundred head of hogs on the land my Dad bought. This fellow had enjoyed

this free range all his life, and he could see no need to move his hogs or buy his own land. It took a lot of persuasion to get him to move his hogs. When he finally moved his hogs from the land, he told my Dad, "You will be sorry you made me move these hogs, because the cabbage trees will take your land." Well, his prophecy has been partially fulfilled on the higher ground, but the lower and wetter areas are still without trees of any kind.

Lack of shade in my pastures led me to purchase a tree spade to transfer cabbage trees from the hammocks located on high ground to open pastures. Cabbage trees should be moved in hot weather, otherwise the heart will be brittle and break during transplanting. I move my cabbage trees without any trimming when they are from six to eight feet tall. They never wilt or show any sign of a setback. They just continue to grow and give instant shade for six to eight cows.

Cabbage trees are an excellent source of stiff fiber. The fiber is in the outer boots on younger trees. In the 1940s, a Mr. John Abney began cutting cabbage palm and shipping them to

Wooten Fiber Company in Jacksonville. The outer boots were removed and processed for the fiber, which made excellent scrub brushes and brooms. Those cabbage trees were cut when they were between six and 10 feet tall. The fans, or branches, were trimmed off and the finished product ready to ship to the factory was approximately 36 to 42 inches in length. Each length averaged 80 to 100 pounds.

To cut the cabbage, Mr. Abney employed a crew of men using wide-bladed axes with razor-sharp edges. Many truckloads were cut off my Dad's land adjoining the Indian reservation. It was a year 'round operation because of the vast area of cabbage hammocks and the fact that new growth was becoming cuttable each year. This new growth is around the edges of the hammocks because the taller trees in the inward hammock shade out the young seedlings.

Mr. Abney also tapped a lucrative market with the sale of cabbage palm spikes, or fronds, which grow out of the middle of the head of the cabbage. They grow out into huge fans. These spikes were cut with a small ax or machete without any harm to the tree. One could be cut from a tree each year. These spikes were cut mostly by the Indians and hauled to Okeechobee, where Mr. Abney bundled them into round rolls of 25. The bundles were then wrapped in burlap to prevent damage during shipping to church supply houses. In bygone years, when the spike business was at its peak, as many as 800,000 were shipped each year. The business has now dwindled to about 150,000 shipped annually.

Churches all over the free world still use and cherish the fronds of cabbage palms for their sacred use in making crosses for Palm Sunday services.

CHAPTER NINE

WHAT IS NO MORE

Early botanists' accounts

Florida is not only graced with spectacular barrier islands all around her coastline, she has inland plant islands as well. Also known as hammocks, these green islands run the length and breadth of the state from the Atlantic Ocean to the Gulf of Mexico. In his 1939 book, *FLORIDA—A Guide to the Southernmost State,* botanist J. K. Small describes a hammock as dense growths of natural trees and shrubs, including cabbage or sabal palms that can occupy a whole circum-scribed portion of a geological formation, or occurring as islands in a sea of piney woods, saw palmetto, or prairie.

Small describes landscapes in northern, central and south-central Florida, where choice hardwoods grow side by side with cabbage palms whose long, broad plume-like fronds brush against the sky, and countless entwining, looping vines such as woodbine, wild grape, morning glory, and miles of Spanish moss festoon the palms and hardwoods alike. And where there is sufficient light, mostly around the perimeter and occasionally where there is open space between inner limbs, there are abundant stands of beauty berry, wild petunia and other wildflowers as well as myriad ferns.

In palm savannas over the entire state, it is the *Sabal palmetto* that prevails. In island clusters or as solitary sentinels, cabbage palms rise straight and tall, almost perfectly symmetrical against Florida's incredible sweep of blue, and stand as etched silhouettes against her scarlet sunrises and sunsets.

Where the terrain is mostly flatland with sand over marl or limestone, growth patterns of the cabbage palm vary widely, from scattered singles in prairies to massive groves of palms with and without oaks. On many of Florida's sun-washed barrier islands, sabal palms have for centuries proven their tenacity in the face of elements. As natural to the islands as the islands are to Florida, *Sabal palmetto* thrives on the green archipelago that spangles Florida's 1,197 miles of coastline.

Nearly a century ago, a man named Hugh L. Willoughby spent almost an entire winter traveling through the Everglades, then published a book detailing his observations and adventures. The trip was, he wrote, "undertaken to explore that unknown portion of the Everglades into which the Seminole Indians were driven during the Indian War. . . also to examine the fauna and flora of the region in the interests of the University of Pennsylvania."

Willoughby's references to the cabbage palm document the way indigenous people used the plant, as well as its role in Florida's natural systems.

In large part, what he observed is no more. The following are excerpts from *Across the Everglades,* the book he published in 1898 about his journey:

About eleven o'clock I sighted an island a little to the left of our course, and by a careful examination with the glass, I could plainly make out a cabbage palm growing from its centre. Now, in any other part of Florida the appearance of a cabbage palm would excite but little interest, as in some places you can see forests of many thousands, but here away out in the Everglades it told a story that gladdened our hearts. It meant dry land. I stopped here to take my usual noon sights, and, though we had made but four miles, we decided to camp on that island. I was sorry that the island could not be reached before the sun crossed the meridian, but did very well without land for my artificial horizon, so after all it made little difference.

I constructed my support in the usual manner by driving three paddles through a few inches of mud to the hard rock bottom, and on the tri-pod so formed inverting a box to obtain a level surface. This was quite as steady as could be desired. On this I placed my black mirror and leveled it. After carefully noting the vernier reading on the sextant and the time by the two chronometers, I set my "back watch" and shaped our course for the island. On a nearer approach a dark gap in the trees was seen, and through it a large clearing and plenty of good high ground. At once we saw that we had struck

a permanent camp and a very old one, too. I jumped ashore at the canoe landing and found the island deserted; but the many objects of interest around incited me to work at once. The island is nearly circular in shape, supporting a heavy growth of timber, matted together near the ground by thick vines. Near the centre, and approached by a cut trail from the eastward, was a clearing about 60 feet in diameter, and like a great tent-pole supporting the canopy of foliage overhead stands the cabbage palm, whose top projects a few feet about the sur-rounding trees and had attracted my attention from the distance. On its trunk a few feet above the ground was a smooth place made with a knife; on this a charcoal drawing of a deer's head and body; at one side a double oval some-what like an elongated figure of eight; beneath and to the right was a figure evidently intended for a squaw; on the left was a hand turned downward. All this is intended to convey some information from one Indian to another. I could not venture upon an interpretation until I should meet some of my Indian friends and describe the place, when, finding that I had visited it, they might be willing to tell me what it signifies.

A hundred years ago [about 1800] there were two other cabbage palmettos growing on this island, which were larger than the central one. I say a hundred, though it may be many more years than that; the fallen trunks were so rotten that merely a shell remained, and in the position I found them a palmetto would keep sound for a very long time. These trees had not fallen by accident, but were cut down when the clearing was made. Over the ground were strewn a dozen shells of the Everglades terrapin, some probably killed a year ago, others almost reduced to dust, showing great age. It is a custom with the Indians to cook this turtle by broiling it before the fire without removing it from the shell. The flesh is really very good and makes quite a savory stew, resembling when carefully prepared the smaller terrapin that bring such high prices in the Northern market. There were many poles scattered about that had been used for shelters and frames for cabbage palmetto

"shacks." At one side of the clearing was a place where the cooking-fire had always been made, and over a large pile of ashes were the charred remains of the last pieces of wood that were used.

On the 19th of January [1897] we were under way at seven o'clock, and the weather being cooler made us feel like putting a good stretch of country behind us. We had not proceeded far before Brewer [a hunter Willoughby had met on his trek] broke the foot of his only pole. As the bottom was all rock here, the accident would not cause any delay, so I tossed him a spare foot, which I carried in my canoe, telling him to put it on in camp that evening. The islands were becoming more frequent, and on many of them there were, no doubt, patches of ground, but we pushed on as long as [we] could see islands ahead that seemed dry. For the first time since leaving Willoughby Key [The author later writes, "'We were in almost the exact centre of the Everglades east and west. I felt for once in my life I had reached ground never before touched by a white man. In my enthusiasm I took my little New York Yacht Club flag from my pocket and Brewer christened the island Willoughby Key."] we saw a cabbage palm, which was a very encouraging sight, as it meant more dry ground. Our noonday meal was rather an unsatisfactory one of cold boiled potatoes. Our biscuit had given out, and I had to try my hand at bread-making over the stove during the evening.

A few better leads were met with the next day, but the water was provokingly shoal, more rock showing itself, over which the grass grew thinly. Long Key lay to the east; the timber on it could be seen occasionally. A very interesting landmark for which I had been steering was a tall palm-tree on a small island. I say interesting, for it was such an uncommon sight to us, and meant not only dry land, but very dry land. The islands were getting closer together, and by three o'clock we made camp on one which seemed especially adapted to our purposes. The water ran close up to it, and from its centre grew two cabbage palms. After the usual clearing was made I cut down one of the cabbage

palms and extracted the cabbage, to form a relish for our evening meal. Very few people, even in Florida, know how delicious the cabbage from the palm can be made. The simplest way is to cut it up raw and use it as cole-slaw; it is tender and has a light nutty flavor. Boiled as ordinary cabbage, it is excellent. In addition to cabbage, this variety of palm bears a black berry about the size of a pea, which resembles a little in flavor the Chinese litchi nut, but the seed is so large in proportion to the nut that many have to be gathered to get much out of them. The heart of the scrub-palmetto can also be used as is the cabbage palm, but many have to be cut and prepared to afford a dish. This camp was by far the best we had made since the one of Willoughby Key, the ground being dry and the water coming well up to the shore, making a short carry for the canoe loads.

The following day we attempted to run on a northeast course, but the water was so low that after many fruitless efforts we decided that we must get more to the eastward, and then followed one of the most exhausting and trying days experienced yet, in which we were out of our canoes nearly all the time; poling was impossible, and dragging for hours became a necessity.

The islands, though small, were high, many of them having several cabbage palms upon them, and so close together that very short compass-bearings could alone be taken. At six o'clock we selected an island and prepared to camp. . . . After a good night's rest we continued our journey, being enabled by the straighter and deeper water-leads to make a better course for the Miami River. . . . At one o'clock we arrived at the camp of Miami Jimmie and the Tiger family that I had visited the previous year. Hardly a sigh remained of the old camp that I remember. A white man had taken possession of the island, driving the Indians away, destroying their Sabal palmetto shacks. . . . On the ruins of the picturesque Indian village, was built an unsightly wooden shanty, and the quadrangle around which the Sabal palmetto dwellings had stood was occupied by a rude vegetable garden.

The foregoing excerpts are from *Across the Everglades* by Hugh L. Willoughby, and appear with the permission of FLORIDA CLASSICS LIBRARY, Port Salerno, Florida, the Florida Classics Library Edition, Copyright 1992.

PART IV
CHAPTER TEN

WORTH THE WAIT

Growing the sabal palm from seed

There is a man in Madison, Florida, who might well consider sabal palms members of his family. After all, Chuck Salter has lived and worked with them all his life. He knows what they like, what they dislike, and he knows how they respond to various growing conditions.

Salter says unequivocally, "The true fact of the matter concerning propagating *Sabal palmetto* is real simple. The cabbage palm grows from seed, and seed only. There is no other way. And if you're in a hurry, you might as well plant something else. A cabbage palm can't be hurried. Only people who are willing to wait—those same people who plant pine trees—should plant sabal palms."

Salter says the main advantage to growing cabbage palms in pots is to make it possible to plant small trees exactly where you want them to grow.

"Small cabbage palms do not tolerate digging and transplanting very well," he says. "By

69

small, I mean palms with no stem or trunk but with fronds from one foot to four feet tall."

Salter's advice on how to successfully grow Florida's state tree from seed comes from his life-long work at Salter Tree Farm in northern Florida. He says sabal palm seeds should be gathered from mature trees in late summer or early fall, preferably when the seed has started to turn black, which is when they germinate the best.

The seeds should be put in a dry place where they should stay until the black outer integument becomes brittle. At this stage, they should be rubbed on hardware cloth to break off the black outer hull, which falls though the screen of the hardware cloth. When the seed has been rubbed on all sides and all the black outer hull has fallen away, the round seed that's left is orange-colored and ready to plant.

For the highest germination rate, seeds should be planted in a tray of 90 percent sand and 10 percent peat, mixed well. Place the tray in light comparable to the forest where sabals grow best—dappled or variable sun and shade. Then wait. And wait. And wait. Without patience, Chuck Salter says, it's difficult to grow sabal palms.

The seeds will sprout in the tray in about three months, sending up a narrow, single green blade. At this point, the thin sprouts should be fertilized with a teaspoon of 20-20-20 soluble fertilizer at one-month intervals.

Keep waiting.

When the green blades have grown to about three inches in height, with a suitable tool, carefully lift the young plants from the tray and transplant them into one-gallon pots. The soil mixture in these pots should be composed of 60 percent sand, 30 percent shredded pine bark about half an inch in size, and 10 percent peat or leaf mold. Water the young palms as needed to keep them slightly moist. Fertilize very lightly in mid-summer. Wait.

Sabal palmetto forms its new leaves, or fronds, in June and July. They do not seem to notice springtime, probably because spring is not a strong season in their natural range.

"Now comes a long wait," says Salter. "The little sabal seedlings develop very slowly. For the next three years, all these little palms want is to be kept slightly moist and to have a light application of fertilizer in mid-summer."

At the end of three years, a couple of the little palms should be lifted out of the pots to see if the roots are crowded. If they are not crowded, they should be replanted in the same pots, after which time more waiting is in store.

However, if the roots are crowded, or pot-bound (and it is likely they will be), the seedlings should be re-potted in three-gallon pots.

And again, wait.

In two more years, at which time the seedlings will be five years old, the root system should be checked again. If crowded, transplant into six-gallon containers.

In its five years of life, the crown of the little sabal palm may only have grown to have three or four fronds 18 to 24 inches across and only two feet tall.

And so, the five-year-old sabal palm is now ready to be safely transplanted into open ground. It will usually start vigorous growth soon after being moved from its containerized world into the soil.

By the time it's 10 years old, it may grow four- to six-foot fronds. And, at about this same time, it will probably form a bud and stem or trunk above ground.

It will take another 10 years, at which time the sabal will be 20 years old, to grow a four-foot stem or trunk with massive six-foot fronds.

"Now," Chuck Salter says, "it should be very clear why very few nurserymen grow cabbage palms in pots," even though, he admits, it's not the maintenance work that's the hard part. "The routine for maintaining life and vigor of palms growing in pots is simple—just follow these rules."

And wait—it's well worth it.

"Look at it his way," Salter concludes. "[At] 1,210 trees per acre. . . [and] even at a 10 percent mortality, the yield will be 1,089 trees in 20 years that will sell for $75 to $95 per tree.

That's a minimum of $81,675.

"Any way this amount of money is looked at, it's a college education, or a dowry in anybody's league!"

TIPS FOR GROWING SABAL PALMS

Sunlight: Cabbage palms are sun-loving, but they also appreciate a little shade. If they are grown in full, open sunlight, they must be watched so that they don't dry out. Cabbage palm feeder roots are very fragile and tender, and dry soil will cause them to dry up and become unable to perform their function— feeding the palm.

Fertilizer: Once or twice in mid-summer, each potted palm should be given one gallon of soluble fertilizer at the rate of one teaspoon per gallon. Here, a basic rule of fertilizing should be noted: Always thoroughly water potted plants prior to applying any fertilizer. If soluble fertilizer is not used, a slow-release granular fertilizer should be applied on top of the soil in the pot at the rate of one tablespoon per pot.

Pests and diseases: Neither pests nor diseases are of great concern, as most insects and diseases seem to greatly prefer other plants; however, once in a while, ants will ascend around the bud and may cause considerable harm. One of the best remedies is to sprinkle any reliable ant powder wherever the ants have congregated. Repeat treatment as necessary.

Also, once in a while, leaf spot can be seen on sabal fronds. Although it does no great damage, the fungus can be controlled with an application of a fungicide.

CHAPTER ELEVEN

TRANSLOCATION

Moving the sabal palm safely

The sabal palm is of vital importance to the lower South's natural ecosystem, so, if for no other reason than that, it should be respected and protected in its natural state. But if that is impossible, instead of bulldozing or burning, all reasonable attempts to move it from harm's way should be made. If minimal demands are met, sabal palms often can be successfully moved if equipment equal to the job is used and if the tree is of the right size. Trees over 10 feet or under three feet tall, if carefully dug with their root ball and replanted, can be moved successfully.

Cabbage palms should be planted deeply in well-prepared soil, preferably during summer months, and watered copiously for a time. Once its roots are cut off, they do not branch. Consequently, the palm must produce new roots from the base following installation. To increase the chances of survival, all fronds should be cut close to the trunk at the time of digging. Newly planted palms should always be supported. After new growth is well under way, the time of which can vary greatly from palm to palm, no more attention will be needed. One who knows how to dig and ship the sabal palm with remarkable success is Terrell Skipper, who owns and operates Statewide Palms in Florida's Hendry County. Skipper regularly sends sabals to many states, including the Carolinas and Texas, and to international destinations as far away as Europe and Mexico. To move *Sabal palmetto* successfully, Skipper says careful handling is critical, as are special attachments that work in conjunction with mechanical tree-moving equipment.

"Several years ago the University of Florida discovered a sure-fire way to assure a 99 percent survival rate of translocated sabal palms," he says. "The root ball must be carefully dug and handled. Then, all the fronds are cut off, including the new growth of the bud but *not the bud itself.* Naturally, since the sabal palm's new growth comes only from the bud, if that is cut the tree will die."

The State of Florida now requires that this method of preparing the tree be followed whenever any sabal palms are moved to government projects. But this has not yet become a mandate for the palm-moving industry.

Skipper says emphatically, "I'd like to see *Sabal palmetto* come under state protection. . . as the state tree [of Florida], it deserves an umbrella of preservation. It's one thing to translocate, but another to 'doz and burn just to clear land."

And he wishes more people knew that their taste for swamp cabbage spells doom for sabal palms. "I'm afraid that most people are unaware that the cabbage palm is killed—absolutely—when the bud is removed," he says thoughtfully. "The state tree of Florida should *not* be harvested like a yearly fruit or vegetable for a mess of swamp cabbage. There's been a lot of misinformation printed about this. . . but fact is fact: when the bud of *Sabal palmetto*, the cabbage palm, is removed for any reason, that palm tree is gone. Killed. And the only way to grow another one is to plant the seed and wait for a lot of years."

CHAPTER TWELVE

BEAUTY BY DESIGN

The Sabal palmetto *in man-made landscapes*

In landscaping, the cabbage palm is highly valued for group plantings, for framing, backgrounds, for avenues and skylines or as a striking solitary focal point. A single sabal palm or a grouping is a natural for the centerpiece of a man-made hammock, particularly when the planting repeats the pattern of the wild, with understory groupings of wax myrtle, dahoon holly, gallberry, saw palmetto and the evergreen fetterbush, with its urn-shaped rosy-pink flowers. In a sense, these trees and plants are "friends," as they thrive together in the same conditions as they have for centuries.

No other palm requires so little in return for so much, thus it is no wonder that *Sabal palmetto* is a favorite in man-made Southern landscapes. Highly tolerant of salt, it grows well in most soils and is happy in either sun or shade or a mixture of both. Almost impervious to heat or cold, most bugs and blights, too much or too little water, the sabal palm has

75

proven itself worthy of an honored position throughout the region.

Another distinct advantage to using sabal palms in landscape design is their great ability to withstand adverse conditions—both man-made and natural—and to steadfastly survive disasters.

Bill Hammond, veteran environmental educator and board member of the South Florida Water Management District, sums it up:

"Often, what is most common is least valued by so many people who flit about in today's urbanizing society. The tragedy with so many of our natural wonders is what was very common in the short yesterdays gone by is today growing uncommon. So it is with the Florida state tree, *Sabal palmetto,* or, to many, the cabbage palm. Each day the sabal palm shrinks in population as habitat is urbanized.

"The sabal is my favorite palm. It is the tree of the beaches, the hammocks, the swamps and marsh edges. It looks good all alone dressed in its boots, or as one of the many forming the damp, cool shade characteristic of the cabbage palm hammock, or as one of the 10 that grow in my residential yard.

"Everyone who can should collect seeds and plant them in his/her yard and speak out against the indiscriminate land-clearing that wastes this wonderfully productive native, which, as a maturing tree even lends itself to successful transplanting (when properly executed) into the landscape of the home, office or commercial setting."

And there's another good reason to landscape with the sabal palm: It's hurricane-hardy. On August 28, 1992, following Hurricane Andrew, a research team from the University of Florida toured urban forest areas with Rick Vasquez, the Metro Dade County Forester. A variety of tree species were observed along streets, in residential areas, in shopping center and commercial areas and in parks. Throughout the entire hurricane-damaged area, *Sabal palmetto* proved to be by far the most resilient tree. Of 284 sabals observed, 261 (92 percent) sustained no noticeable damage, 12 had broken trunks and

11 had minor leaf damage. These results were later published in *Hurricane Andrew Damage to the Urban Forest: A Preliminary Evaluation.*

The sabal palm's virtues have not been lost on the entertainment business. Several truckloads of Florida sabals recently found a glamorous new home in Branson, Missouri, a live show entertainment district known to some as "the new Nashville," where country and western stars have filled the town with theaters and music halls. Several semi-truckloads of sabals now add their own very southern charm to the country music landscape.

Although there are diverse opinions as to the success of planting sabals deeper than their natural ground level, (20-year records from Lee County, Florida, indicate that fill dirt piled around the trunk, even up to six feet high, does not affect the sabal's natural growth. Although Dr. Alan W. Meerow, an associate professor and palm specialist from the University of Florida, says, "We've seen sabals decline from this practice. It may take

five or 10 years, however.")

It may be that the cabbage palm is perhaps the only tree that can tolerate being planted at any depth without harm.

In any case, when palms are situated in groups, it is more naturally pleasing to see them at varying heights. Mother Nature dramatically demonstrates this principle in natural hammocks—a landscape design that usually begins with seeds for one or two trees carried in animal droppings. As time goes on, wild creatures seek food and refuge in the first tree or trees, then others spring up close by, other wild plants begin to grow in their shelter, and a hammock is in the making.

One of the early champions of the idea of planting the *Sabal palmetto* in hammocks—and of planting sabal palms in general—was Florida botanist Dr. Henry Nehrling. In the decades from the early 1890s until his death in 1929, he produced a series of horticultural articles for *The American Eagle* newspaper in Estero, Florida, many of which celebrated the state's palms. In "The Cabbage Palmetto," he wrote:

Though avenues of palmettos are wonderfully charming, I prefer natural groves or groups as we find them in our woodlands. Wherever they are, they should be carefully preserved. Frequently we come upon large assemblages of Palmettos, forming large forests by themselves with no other tree among them and with scarcely any underwood. Their leaves meet overhead, the light is obscure, and when we look upward it seems as if we had entered a dome or a cathedral. . . .

It may be safely said that . . . many residents of Florida never have cast their eyes upon a real Palmetto forest. . . . There ought to be avenues and large groups and groves of cabbage Palmettos in every hamlet and town. We in this congenial Southland should not live in dreary, bleak, forlorn-looking homesteads, when Nature supplies us so bountifully with the most impressive and charming plants in existence. . . . The Cabbage Palm is one of our most striking and valuable assets. It should take the lead everywhere.

THE *SABAL PALMETTO* IN MAN-MADE LANDSCAPES
by Teresa Artuso

The allure of the Florida lifestyle comes from not only a glorious, subtropical climate and luxurious beaches, but from a horticultural extravaganza in the landscape as well. Mild temperatures and seasonal, heavy rains create a lush landscape palette, rich with beautiful possibilities.

In today's environmentally conscious society, the need for water conservation is encouraged. When looking for drought-tolerant species and those "most likely to succeed," native plants often come to mind. It makes good sense to use natives, as they are "tried and true," having stood the test of time in our environment's soil and climate conditions.

For water conservation, landscape interest and longevity, *Sabal palmetto* is a sound, intelligent choice. It is unsurpassed for roadside planting, highway beautification and commercial and residential landscaping. Along the beachfront, the cabbage palm is an excellent choice to withstand the harsh effects of salt spray and strong winds.

Aside from obvious ecological reasons, the use of native plants is important in creating a timeless essence and a sense of permanence. The cabbage palm, saw palmetto, oaks, pines, etc., are part of the traditional landscape and lend a historic character to present-day development. Because of its tall, regal stature, the cabbage palm is often used for architectural enhancement, to soften corners or blank facades and to reduce the scale of a building or residence. This effect makes the structure feel "nestled in," established and less newly constructed. From a budgetary standpoint, the cabbage palm is often chosen because several trees can be planted in a cluster for less expense than other single species. As the state tree of both Florida and South Carolina, *Sabal palmetto* has been given a place of honor throughout the native environment. It deserves a similar place of honor throughout the man-made environment as well.

Landscape architect Teresa Artuso is president of the site planning and landscape architectural firm of Burner & Company, of Southern Florida and Northern California.

CHAPTER THIRTEEN

RESTORATION OR PRESERVATION?

Saving the sabal palm

Although it can be found throughout the lower Southern states in a variety of habitats, increasing threats to wild-growing *Sabal palmetto* are evident: large-scale clearing of both adult and immature trees from development sites—despite "replacement mandates"—a high mortality rate from relocation efforts, and the continued harvesting of swamp cabbage, a practice that sacrifices the life of the tree for a small portion of food that today is little more than a novelty.

Not only is the sabal palm at the mercy of the clearing saws and bulldozers of developers, and the axes and machetes of swamp cabbage-seekers, there are growing indications that it is also at the mercy of rising underground saltwater levels, particularly along Florida's Gulf Coast in the region of Cedar Key to Homosassa Springs, especially in the Wacasassa Bay area. To a lesser degree, dying sabals have also been documented near Tampa Bay and Jacksonville. And aerial surveys conducted by the state's forestry division have identified hundreds of thousands of distressed sabal palms.

According to Florida's Agricultural Commissioner, Bob Crawford, the state's first course of action was to determine if pests or diseases were responsible for the die-off. But after pathologists eliminated insects, other pests or diseases as possible causes, the state's investigators turned to the University of Florida. There, researchers in the departments of botany and forestry have pointed to changing environmental conditions as the likely cause of the problem.

"The University's preliminary findings indicate a rising salt water level as the likely culprit," says Commissioner Crawford.

Although the research is ongoing, it is believed that as the state's population and demand for water has increased, levels in the underground freshwater aquifers have dropped more quickly than they are being naturally recharged. As a result, saltwater can seep in to fill the void, and this saltwater intrusion can harm plants.

While the sabal palm is widely assumed to be so abundant as to not be under any pressure, the fate of the region's cypress trees may be instructive: Not more than 50 years ago, Florida's cypress trees were in great abundance; very old, very large cypress trees were ordinary. It wasn't unusual to find trees 400 to 600 years old, up to eight feet in diameter above the buttress.

It was commonly thought that there was enough cypress for everyone, for every purpose. So the giant cypress trees were cut and cut and cut until they became rare indeed. Now—after the fact—federal wetland laws and some local tree ordinances offer some measure of protection.

There are unsettling parallels between the cypress and the sabal palm: The sabal palm's growth is deliberate and slow, as is that of the cypress. The sabal palm seems to grow in lavish, unending abundance. But at one time, there were more cypress trees than sabal palms.

We who love and cherish the original nature

of the South—unaltered—must not allow the cabbage palm, a natural treasure of the region, to be destroyed.

Sabal palmetto, along with the small, wondrous world of wild creatures and plants of which she is the center, is vital to this glorious land, whose fragile natural systems have been pitifully damaged.

There was a time when pink flamingoes flew here, when panthers roamed and mammoth cypress trees stood silently on the southern swamps. And in Florida, there was the magnificent, meandering Kissimmee River that unerringly and faithfully fed life-sustaining rainwater through natural grasslands to Lake Okeechobee and to the Everglades.

As we move through the last decade of the twentieth century, the cabbage palm still grows widely throughout the region. Yet, there are numerous areas where it is no more.

Unless we cry *Stop!* and demand that our voices be heard, the sabal palm's fate will inevitably join that of the pink flamingoes, the panthers, the giant cypress and the once-pristine Kissimmee.

Restoration can never equal preservation.

CONCLUSION

The stoic *Sabal palmetto* stands as the matriarch across the Florida landscape. Her existence is harmonious with the hills and riverbeds of Northern Florida and the languid lake edges of its central plains. She dances across the coastal dunes or hides in the hammocks of the southern areas of the state. Etched into the pictorial landscape, she evokes the character and quality of Florida, nurturing the environment.

It is important to acknowledge her noble position amidst the ecological structure of the natural landscape. She plays a major part in the Florida wildlife, providing food, fiber and shelter to the worlds hidden from the urban environment. Her symphonic association with other plant species creates unique micro-climates. These ecological systems are diverse and varied, supporting and perpetrating life, yet coexisting in harmony.

As our human habitat expands, we have domesticated this versatile survivor who has gained respect in the urban landscape. As the South Carolina and Florida state tree, man has acknowledged her role. But man bullishly abuses what nature has created in perfect balance. This palm plays an integral part in the orchestration of the most magnificent symphony of nature, the fragile symphony that has been playing for thousands of years.

Peter B. Burner

A Florida native, Peter B. Burner is a landscape architect who received the Nurseryman's National Landscape Award for Excellence in 1992 at the White House.

EPILOGUE

The evolutionary processes that shape plant communities and tie one life form to another have been in place since the beginning of time. Whether or not the human animal understands or appreciates how these processes work is really unimportant to the success of the system. Life will continue on this planet whether people are included or not.

So, who cares? Well, the human animal should. How well we understand the workings of nature and direct our collective behavior will dramatically affect how we are treated by natural systems. If we control our own population, nature won't have to evolve new diseases to control it for us. If we maintain biodiversity, natural systems will continue to provide life support benefits that make this plan-

et a comfortable place to live.

Though life has been on this planet for billions of years, we, the more highly developed human animal, have been here for only a blink of the eye in geologic time. How long we remain here is totally up to us. If we maintain the functioning natural systems upon which our existence depends, we may well remain here as long as some of the lower life forms.

If all of this is to happen, it is essential that people better appreciate how important quality natural systems are to us. It really isn't important that we fully understand all the functions of nature but only that we allow it to continue to function.

Less than 100 years ago in Florida, people lived more closely with cabbage palms and other natural systems components. W. S.

Blatchley, a winter visitor to Florida in 1911, recorded many of his field experiences with native plants. He also wrote about how people living in the Florida "primeval wilderness" interacted with native plants. Blatchley, an entomologist, shared his Florida encounters with insects and people in his book *In Days Agone,* published in 1932.

On Monday, February 20, 1911, Blatchley wrote about the first time he experienced *Sabal palmetto* "cabbage" as food. "Anything used for food by other humans I am always willing to try once," he wrote, "Cooked as one does cauliflower by boiling and properly seasoned, it was very edible but without much taste."

During his trip, Blatchley and his naturalist companions spent much of their time foraging. They collected and ate ducks, fish, oysters, fruit, berries and hearts of cabbage palms. They always took more than they needed— Florida's riches seemed inexhaustible.

If Blatchley could return to Florida today, he would find that indeed there is an end to the Florida wilderness. Cabbage palms nor any other component of Florida's natural systems can be treated as if there is no end to the supply.

Having looked closely at the cabbage palms, just one of Florida's 3,448 plants, we find that there is quite an interesting web of life connected to this species. This magnificent palm is one component of complex natural systems that enable South Florida to function.

It will be interesting to see if we can appreciate the cabbage palm for its role in those natural systems' function. It will also be interesting to see if we can appreciate how dependent we are on collectively developing that appreciation and behaving accordingly.

Florida's natural systems must be treated as if our lives depended on their continued function. To do otherwise is to abandon any respect for the generations of people and other creatures of nature that will follow.

Fort Myers, Florida, biologist Richard Workman is the author of Growing Native *and a founding member of the Florida Native Plant Society.*